101

Black Pearls
of Wisdom

From the Sermons
Of Bishop W. Oshea Granger

Compiled by V. Lynn Whitfield

Published by
Emerge Publishing Group, LLC
Riviera Beach, FL
www.emergepublishers.ccm

Printed in the United States of America

Table of Contents

Preface

How often have you attended church and listened intently to the message? Perhaps you have taken notes and filled journal after journal for the purpose of going back later and reviewing what was preached. But have you ever gone back and looked over those notes? Or do they sit collecting dust?

Since 1997, I have written down sermon notes from one of the greatest pastors/teachers I know. I promised to go back and review them, but never did. Then on Christmas morning, 2009, the Lord gave me a divine assignment to compile this book of pearls of wisdom I have obtained listening to the sermons of my pastor–Bishop W. Oshea Granger.

This started as a Christmas/Birthday gift for him, to let him know that I do listen and learn from his sermons. It has developed into much more. It is my prayer that whosoever reads this book will be blessed by the words and the

message. It is also my prayer that the proceeds from the sale of this book will bless young people as they seek a higher education and a closer walk with God.

Presented with Love to all who have been fed by the Word.

V. Lynn Whitfield

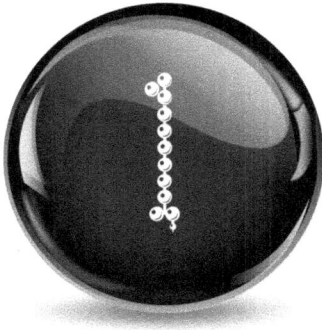

The opportunity of a
lifetime must be seized
in the lifetime of
the opportunity.

Don't put

limitations on

God's promises.

There are some things that God has purposed for you that sin, satan, self and/or society stop you from receiving. But there are some things He has not subjected to any of those things and are within His power alone.

If you have a mindset

to endure then you

can be an Overcomer.

5

If you trust God
on the small stuff,
your life will not
unravel on the
big stuff.

God gives us gifts

we don't even know

to ask for ourselves.

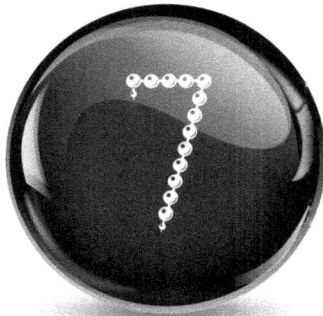

If you really want to

learn about faith, put

yourself in the position

of adversity–you will learn

lessons that will stay

with you your whole life.

You will never
be tempted by
something you
don't want.

God determines how strong you are before He allows things to come your way.

Your ability to
handle future crisis
is built up by the
memory of your
past crisis.

Real worship can be easy

even at your darkest

hour—but you don't wait

until the dark hours come

to decide it's now time

to worship God.

Worship can
move the hand
of God.

If you learn to
pray in the calm
you can play
in the storm.

13

14

You can't have
your way if you
are going to allow
God to have His.

15

Stop looking at
how things are
and look at what
God said things
will be.

15

Don't be satisfied
with things being as
well as it is, when as
well as it is, is not as
good as it could be.

17

Because you have
suffered some things,
you now know how much
courage you have.

Don't measure me
by the size of my trials,
tribulations or temptations;
measure me by the
God inside me.

It may take you
down, but don't
let it take you out.

It doesn't get

any better than

trusting God.

21

Sometimes the blessing God has for you is tied to what He has already made.

22

Whatever God

says—is what

you better do.

23

It is one thing

to hear God

it is another

to heed God.

24

God obligates us
to share our
experience with
those coming behind us.

If church is
important—some
of your money
will be going there.

You will only live

once in this world

so make your life

count for what

is important.

27

Everybody should be too busy to do something at church sometime, but nobody should be so busy that they never have any time to do something at church sometime.

28

You sell yourself
short when you fail
to realize that there
is more to you
than just you.

29

You can't use
up God's peace.

Don't lose sight
of whatever it is
that God has
promised you.

Don't get so
caught up in trying
to compete with
others that you
miss your assignment.

32

Only depend on
people whose faith
will take you as
far as you need
to go—all the way.

Love

is as

Love does.

Be careful

who you let

handle you.

Don't become

dependent on

people who don't

believe in

your future.

36

When God
choose you
it is not because
of you.

There ain't no shortcuts

for you getting

from where you

are to the place God

wants you to be.

Whatever you have

came from

God-man is just

the agent who

brought it to you.

If you don't know
the principles and
promises of God,
you can't enjoy the
prosperity of God.

Bondage can

be traced to

your taste.

Some will not

secure the blessing

because they

can't get over

the source.

God will put

marks all over you.

People will

recognize you as

a child of God.

People can do
what appears to
be a good thing
but do it with
a bad spirit.

You can't buy

anointing

or spirituality.

It is important to praise people for what they are worthy to be praised for doing.

45

Hurt people,

hurt people.

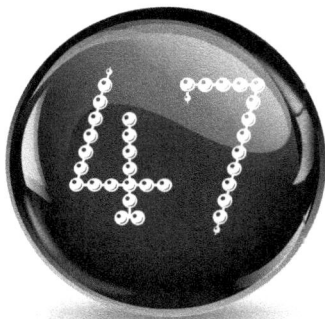

47

You can have

a handicap, but

the handicap does

not have to

have you.

47

God never runs

out of what you

are in need of.

When you do
what you do well,
you showboat
the glory of God.

49

Do not let

your handicap

effect your direction.

Sometimes to get
to the place God
wants us to be,
we have to stay
in the place He
causes us to be kept.

52

The worth of what
God has promised
you will be revealed
by what you will
pay for it.

53

EGO

means – Edging

God Out.

God uses people
to unlock the
mysteries that show
us a side of ourselves
we didn't know we had.

55

You will always
gain by investing
in the future
of others.

You have got
to believe that
God is going to
do something
when you pray.

57

Even in bad

times you

are blessed.

God can find

you wherever

you are because

God knows

your voice.

59

When you want
to find pleasure
in the world, learn
to fall in love with
the law of the Lord.

Your mind is a
gateway to the
sum total of
who you are.

Don't let the
devil have more
power than
you have.

You have got to
get to the point where you
can talk about what God has
done for you. You should
have a personal story.

63

Because of the tender mercies of God, you can have inner satisfaction.

It is up to you
what you do
with the potential
God gives you.

65

You have to humble
yourself to get
down to Jesus.
Sometimes you have
to get on your knees.

66

When life beats you down;
when things get to you;
when people get under your
skin~Jesus will come and
will give you a Word that
changes your circumstances.

When Jesus showed
His wounds, He was
demonstrating the
ultimate transparency.

68

If you are a
disciple of Christ,
you have to believe
that if Jesus made it
through, you will too.

69

Don't be in
denial—accept
the reality of
the times.

Worry and panic
do not take away
any pain from tomorrow;
all they do is take
away the joy of today.

71

The past should
not be the measuring
stick to determine
your future.

You have to be
inspired, encouraged
and empowered to
develop the strategy
to go where God
will take you.

73

You have to get
to the place where you
decide that this is
worth fighting for.

74

It does not take
anything away
from you to bless
someone else.

75

Don't come just
to show up–but
come to show out.

76

You should have
a sense of gratitude
because of all that
God has done
for you.

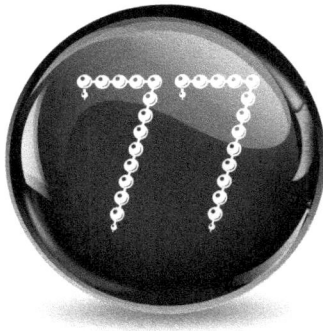

Stop waiting
for promotion
and start working
for production.

78

You can never be
a winner if you
allow yourself to
be overcome by fear.

Reflect credit
away from you
and give credit
where due–to God.

Make up your

mind to take

the first step.

80

Declare your

desired outcome.

82

God wants to
move us to the
place where we
trust Him and
not ourselves.

You can't

conceal yourself

from God.

Prayer – confer
with Him
Praise – convey
to Him
Repentance – confess
to Him
Call on Him.

No matter where
you are~you
can't lock Jesus
out of your life.

Picture getting
something positive
from surviving
something negative.

There are limits
placed on what
the devil can do
in your life.

God can make
more with His
fingers than we
can do with every
part of our bodies.

God cares more

about souls

than He does

about stars.

As members become
better Christians,
we become a
better Church.

91

You've got to deal with it from the inside—let yourself be made what you ought to be.

92

Pay attention
to the fundamentals.

Being a Christian is not a guarantee that good things are going to happen in your life—but being a Christian is a guarantee that no matter what happens in your life God will be faithful.

When God loves
you~He
loves you
just right.

95

Don't plan for
bad things to
happen, but have
a plan when they do.

96

Excuses are the skills of incompetence which builds monuments of nothing and people who practice them accomplish nothing else.

97

There will always

be someone

listening for what

you have to say.

If you want to
be chosen for the Glory of
God, your mindset should be
what can I do to give God
glory instead of what can I
do to satisfy man.

Delay is not

a denial.

You can't have
so many trials
in your life that
they out number
the peace of God.

Why worry

when you

can pray.

101

Thank You

*A special thank you to **Bishop Walter Oshea Granger** for all his words of inspiration and the guidance he gives to the members of his congregation every week.*

May God continue to bless him and give him a double anointing as he feeds God's people.

About the Bishop

Bishop W. Oshea Granger
www.mcbcwpb.org

Bishop Granger is the senior pastor at Mt. Calvary Baptist Church, West Palm Beach, Florida. He is also the Regional Bishop for the Southeast Region of the Full Gospel Baptist Fellowship. He is both a gifted preacher and teacher of the Word of God. His sermons have had a profound impact on all who have been blessed to hear them. Remember faith comes from hearing the Word.

About the Author

V. Lynn Whitfield has been a member of Mt. Calvary Baptist Church for over ten years. She has been taking notes from the sermons of Bishop Granger the entire time and was inspired by God to compile this collection as a tribute to God and her pastor. It is her desire that the pearls of wisdom in this book will touch the hearts of each reader and enrich their lives as they have hers.